ACTORS WRITE FOR ACTORS

A Collection of Original Audition Monologues

Written by
**JASON MILLIGAN
DEBORAH COWLES SCOTT
ROBERT SPERA**

SAMUEL FRENCH, INC.
45 WEST 25TH STREET   NEW YORK 10010
7623 SUNSET BOULEVARD HOLLYWOOD 90046
LONDON   TORONTO

To Jon Jory and Actors Theatre of Louisville

FORWARD

Having all worked as actors — and, more importantly, having *sought* work as actors — we are fully aware that the selection of monologues available from published plays is quite limited and the best pieces are more often than not overdone.

Our intent in creating this book is to provide fresh material to the now-existing body of audition pieces available to the actor.

Hence, here's *Actors Write For Actors.* Very simply, we've acknowledged a need and we've tried to supply a varied selection of material for all types. We've had a great time writing these pieces and we hope you'll have a great time working on them.

Break-a-leg!

Jason Milligan
Deborah Cowles Scott
Robert Spera
New York, July 1986

THE MONOLOGUES

MEN

President by Jason Milligan
Living Together by Robert Spera
Mailman by Robert Spera
Kids by Jason Milligan
Editorial by Robert Spera
Thank God For Rational Thinking by Jason Milligan
The Home by Jason Milligan
Going Back by Jason Milligan
Attention! by Robert Spera
Summer Camp by Jason Milligan
Till Death Do Us Part by Robert Spera
Blue Detergent by Jason Milligan
Powder-Keg by Jason Milligan
Harvard Blues by Jason Milligan
Tit-Man by Jason Milligan
Travels by Jason Milligan
Man of Action by Jason Milligan
Impulsive Nature by Robert Spera
College Hill by Jason Milligan
For Dad by Jason Milligan
Boxer's Nightmare by Robert Spera
Goldfish by Robert Spera
Cure For the Curse of the Lonely Guy by Jason Milligan
The Suggs Saga by Jason Milligan

WOMEN

Precarious Position by Deborah Cowles Scott
The Sea of Life by Jason Milligan
Picture Postcards by Deborah Cowles Scott
A Tribute to Real Men by Deborah Cowles Scott

THE MONOLOGUES

WOMEN
(continued)

Please by Jason Milligan
Stress by Deborah Cowles Scott
The Proposal by Robert Spera
30 Years Too Late by Jason Milligan
True Love by Deborah Cowles Scott
Hot Dog by Jason Milligan
Unexpected by Deborah Cowles Scott
Dating by Jason Milligan
Unemployment by Deborah Cowles Scott
Special by Jason Milligan
Date Book by Jason Milligan
From the Heart by Jason Milligan
Mother by Name by Deborah Cowles Scott
Place by Jason Milligan
Liberated 80's by Deborah Cowles Scott
Problems by Jason Milligan
And Justice For All by Deborah Cowles Scott
Too Honest by Jason Milligan
People by Jason Milligan

MEN

PRESIDENT

I fall in love 20, maybe 30 times a day on the subway. Beautiful women in this town, only you can't sit there and look at 'em cause if they catch you doin' it they think you're some kinda pervert or somethin' and they give ya the cold stare. You know, the COLD STARE? Yeah. Well, it's tough bein' nobody, you end-up starin' at all the beautiful women and none of 'em ever wind-up starin' back. So I figure, if they knew our faces — and correct me if I'm wrong here, Rob — then they WILL stare back; cause they'll wonder who WE are for a change. So what I wanna do here, Rob, is for us to run for President! You for President, me for Vice-President. And — see, not cause I really wanna WIN or anything, shit no. But to get our faces on those CAMPAIGN POSTERS all over the city! You know, all the light poles and phone booths and everywhere? And then they'd have no CHOICE but to recognize us when we look at 'em on the subway and if they deduce that we're like, you know, POLITICAL MAGNATES, they'll want to stare back! Who knows? If we play our cards right, we might not only get stared at, we might even get LAID!

LIVING TOGETHER

Okay! Hold it right there. Get your finger out of your nose. Come on! Get it out. Look Ginny, I'm serious. It's disgusting. It would be one thing if you were two but you're twenty-seven. Oh, and don't tell me you were scratching your nose. This is scratching. *(He demonstrates.)* Your index finger was buried up to the knuckle. Listen, we have to be careful. I mean, living together like this. We can't take each other for granted. You can't get too familiar and think it's okay to pick your nose in front of me. Next thing you'll be belching and farting. It doesn't show any goddamned respect for me. Take my word for it. That's what ruined my first marriage. That lack of respect eroded our relationship. Not only that but it's plain old goddamned disgusting and it grosses me out. Everytime you touch me all I can think of is booger finger. Now please, from now on, no more nose picking. Believe me, it starts out as picking but it ends in divorce.

MAILMAN

Sometimes the simplest things can change your life. How long have I been working at Consolidated? Ten years? Well for ten years the mailman has walked into my office and dropped the mail on the desk. We've exchanged the same obligatory remarks for ten years. Never changes: "Hey, having a good morning?" "Eh, so-so. How about you?" "Eh, so-so." Every day, ten years. Today he walks in and says, "Hey, in case I don't see you, take it easy! Today is my last day, I'm retiring." I say, "Yeah, well, take it easy." Then I realized I didn't even know his name — ten years. Never really getting to know this man. Then I started thinking about you and me. I think I've done the same thing with you. Just passing the time. Obligatory remarks, just say and do what we have to do to get by. Never investing too much or too little. Just enough to get by. Just passing time. I realized I didn't know who you are and it scared me. You could walk in and say you were screwing the next door neighbor's dog and I'd have to believe it. I don't know you. I've been in a fog.

KIDS

I do too! I think about kids! I think about kids a lot! It's always in the back a my head. And sometimes it's good things I think about and sometimes it's not so good and sometimes it's just plain scary. I mean, really scary. I was looking at this milk carton the other day at breakfast — you had already left — and on the back side, there was these pictures of a little boy and a little girl. And right over their heads, it says "Missing Children" in bright red letters. And I looked at the picture of the little girl real close ... really LOOKED at her ... and I thought, "This is SOMEbody's kid. It's not just a picture; it's somebody's kid." I thought, what if that little girl was mine? Ours? How would we be feeling, having something like that happen and having it so PUBLIC and having to deal with it EVERY SINGLE DAY? I probably sound like a raving lunatic but I couldn't get that picture outta my head. So much to think about with kids. It's like, you got your job and I got mine and between us we got forty million things to worry about. But if we go through with this — and I'm not saying I DON'T WANT to — then we got a hundred million things to worry about. I swear, there's nothing I want more than to be a father. It used to be being your husband, and that's still first place. It's just — I'm scared. I know you want this. I do too, honey. Just ... bear with me. Please. I'll do my best to get over these bullshit insecurities of mine. Just ... bear with me.

EDITORIAL

Hey, enough with these fucking Libyans or Siberians or Syrians or whoever the fuck they are. They're getting to be a pain in the ass, that's what I say. How can we let a country the size of Brooklyn bust our balls like this? I tell you one thing: the Mafia wouldn't stand for this shit. I mean, the frigging Mafia would say, "Hey Kadaffy, suck on *this!*" Bingo. No more problems. You know, we should just go in there and blow them out of the fucking water. I mean, level the fucking place. Then when the smoke clears just sweep all that shit into the ocean and start over. You know, like relocate a whole fucking town from Indiana. You know, good people. I mean, if these bozos can't knock it off, we should just blow them off the face of the map and replace them with some other people. People you can talk to. Hell, move Brooklyn there. Open up a few pizza parlors, coupla clam bars, a nice pastry shop, coupla casinos and you're back in business. You know what I mean. You gotta let these people know. Hell, nobody's fucking indispensable. That's what I say.

THANK GOD
FOR RATIONAL THINKING

Okay. Let's stick to the facts here. The basic problem here is I don't know what to GET her. It's her birthday party and I have no IDEA what to get her. If it were any OTHER situation, I'd know just what to do, see, but HE invited me to her goddamn birthday party! So let's stick with the facts here. I could get her a bottle of wine or roses — NO! I can't get her roses! I mean, she's MARRIED, for chrissakes! I guess that's step one. Good. Yeah. Admit the facts: I am in love with a maried woman. Good. Okay. Let's stick with the facts: I am totally, completely, insanely infatuated with this woman and she's married. Good. Facts. And she's got a husband. WHO'S A NICE GUY! I mean, it'd be different if he was an asshole or something, but no — he's a nice guy! Invited me to this goddamn party! Jerk! Okay, stick with the facts here: I am madly in love with a woman who has a nice husband and he wants to get me drunk and STRANGLE me at this party. He knows. He MUST know. I stare at her all the time! Okay. Facts. This may very well be the last night of my life here. So I might as well get her a good present and go out in style. Good. Five dozen red roses. That's what I'll get her. Five dozen red roses. *(beat)* Thank God for Rational Thinking!

THE HOME

Mom, I can't keep doing this. I can't. I just ... can't anymore. You call me and I'm supposed to drop whatever I'm doing and drive out here .... I've got my own business now, Mom. I can't be leaving like that. For a calendar. Or a *TV Guide*. Or a can of soup. A damn can of soup you call me for. Well, there it is, why don't you eat it? *(beat)* Well, I am sorry if I made you lose your appetite. Mom, you just gotta face the way things are. It was DIFFERENT ten years ago. FIVE years ago. They used to deliver this stuff for you, remember? Old Man Fudge and his boys. But he's out of business now, Mom. There's a supermarket now and I'm the only one around who can bring you things. And ... I got other stuff now, Mom. I got a WIFE now, Mom, I — *(beat) Mom, stop playing in the soup. Mom, I can't keep it up. I WON'T. Marie deserves as much of me as you do and she's not getting it. Look. (pause)* I picked up these ... brochures ... this week. I want you to look at 'em. It's a nice place, Mom. I drove out there Thursday. I think you'd be happy there, and it's not like we wouldn't come see you. It's only 45 minutes away, you KNOW we'd come see you. *(pause)* I know you don't want to do this and I swear to God I don't want to either. Mom ... I love you, you know that. You know I do. But there's just no other way. Please think about it, Mom. Please say you will. Just think it over. For me.

GOING BACK

Shit, I tried; but I didn't stay in touch with any of 'em too well. I called Joey a couple of times. Wrote Nicky once or twice. It's hard, once you leave. You know? You got new people, new things in your life. Anyway, so I went to our big High School reunion party last night. Five years? Yeah, and I'm thinkin, five years ain't that long, y'know. Shit, you got any idea how much things can change in five years? And by that I don't mean THEM; Joey was still hanging-out on that same old stool at Ireland's. Nicky was still on the car lot, still wearing a plaid sportcoat. Not the same sportcoat, but still, the same old shit. Y'know? It wasn't them that changed so much as what was BE-TWEEN me and them. Oh, hell, it was great to see 'em all and all that. Really. But after a few drinks, we had covered all the old ground and the new ground was — well, sorta like a frozen pond. You don't know how thick the ice is; you don't know if it's safe to walk on and maybe you step onto the ice and it ain't thick enough and SPLASH! You go through into the cold water. And shit, that water I'm talkin' about can be pretty fuckin' cold. I thought it was all gonna be the same. I wanted so bad for it to be the same. But I guess ... it can't be.

ATTENTION!

Good morning, Gentlemen. *(pause)* I said, Good Morning, Gentlemen. *(Pause)* Thank you. My name is Sergeant Richardson. I am very pleased to meet all of you. You'll find out pretty quickly that I run things a little differently than you expected. What I have just handed-out to you are standard army-issue vinyl body bags. Major function: corpse transportation. I even took the liberty of having your names embossed in gold on the outside. I know it's a little premature, but I've found it saves time later. Because let's face facts, Gentlemen. Two out of three of you will be coming back in one of those bags. Sad but true. Now, the way I see it, by late this afternoon I will begin to get on your nerves. By tomorrow morning, you will learn to hate me, and by Friday — you will want to kill me. But that's okay, because six months from now in the the middle of a firefight, you will pledge your undying love for me. Now, I bet you expected me to yell and scream at you for eight weeks. But the way I see it, you either listen to me real closely — that's right, strain your ear muscles to hear what I have to say — or you can start unzipping your bags right now. *(pause)* Enjoy your first day here. At ease.

SUMMER CAMP

God, I hate this place. I hate these kids. I *really* hate these kids. I thought, before I came here, that they'd be wild some of the time. But I thought they'd behave too. Aw, they don't *ever* behave. I have to keep track of this whole damn cabin-full of kids. All by myself. And they're always losin' stuff or gettin' hurt, or — HEY! Put that down! Put it DOWN! You're gonna poke your eye out, you keep playin' with that. Listen to me! Put it DOWN! *(pause)* Y'see that? It's always like that. Y'know, it's like they know I hate 'em. And they do stuff like that just to piss me off, know what I mean? Jerry, don't put that in your mouth. I don't care what they did on TV, just don't do it, okay? Jerry, will you — Jerry? Good. That's good. *(pause)* I wouldn't be here now if it weren't for Caroline. You remember Caroline, don't you? With the *hair?* Yeah, well *she* was the one, wanted to WORK here together. Okay, fine. So I stay here. Man, she walks OUT on me. I busted my ass for her, I did anything she wanted. Left me for a damn ... arcade manager. So. Here I am. Camp Fucking Yoc'na. I call it Yech-na. Makes the staff mad. Hey — do you smell something burning? *(Looks around, sees something.)* Wait a minute. I'll be right back.

TILL DEATH DO US PART

Shh! Shhh! Come over here. I don't want to talk in front of the desk. I think it's bugged. Seriously. Now listen to me carefully. You gotta help me. I think my life is in danger. No, seriously. I think Debbie is KGB. Look, I know this sounds crazy, I know she's only 22 and she's the cutest little button of a thing from Kentucky. Yes, she's a former high school cheerleader and she was president of the Homecoming Float Committee. But we've lost her. She's gone under. She's KGB. She's a perfect candidate. No one would ever suspect her. Call it a hunch if you have to. It all started after our vacation to Romania last summer. I think they recruited her over there. Ever since then, she's been acting strange. Sometimes in the morning, I hear her talking to herself in the bathroom. I think she's sending some kind of signals from there. She never used to lock the bathroom door before and now she locks it all the time. You gotta help me. I think she's trying to kill me. I'm afraid to eat her cooking. Well, I know I've always been afraid to eat her cooking, but this is different. I'm afraid to go to sleep at night. I woke up once last week and I caught her looking at me wierd. Then, last night, I heard this wierd sound in the bedroom. I did some research and there is this kind of dart gun that explodes in a mist in your face and it kills you instantly, but in the autopsy it looks like you had a heart attack. All day long I've had this funny feeling in my chest. You gotta help me. I can't eat and I can't sleep. I know I have a history of paranoia but that was germs and shit. This is different. This is the goddamned KGB. They're everywhere. And they got my Debbie. Oh, Debbie. Look, if I die of a heart attack, I want you to hunt her down and kill her. Will you do that for me, Bennie?

BLUE DETERGENT

This is a kennel, Dan. A goddamn kennel. They let us out for din-din. They reward us if we've been good ... they PUNISH us if we've been bad ... it's just like a kennel. This job has total control over us. We have NO individuality, Dan. We are JUST LIKE DOGS! It wasn't until last night that I realized that, Dan. How controlled we are. I met this girl, Dan, and she — I mean — you cannot BEGIN to realize ... what last night WAS for me! It was like that TV Commercial. You know, that TV Commercial, the one about laundry detergent? You haven't seen it. Well, there's this baseball player guy on there — and he's really stupid, but that's not the point. The point is, his suit is all dirty and they wash it in this blue detergent and all of a sudden it's sparkling and white and NEW! And this guy, who you think is such a loser, he wins the SERIES! And that's how I feel! I'm that baseball player's uniform! I feel sparkling and white and new! Oh, and soft. I feel really ... kinda soft inside. Shit, Dan, we gotta enjoy ourselves! What the hell are we *here* for anyway, huh? Not so we can get treated like dogs, boy, that's for sure! So I am turning in my resignation, Dan. And if you wanna stay here and answer to these sons of bitches, fine, okay. But I am gonna kick back and enjoy myself for a change. I just hope ... that sooner or later, you'll find the blue detergent that makes your uniform white.

POWDER-KEG

You know me, Chas. I've had spring fever since fuckin'
NOVEMBER. Maybe I'm just too wound-up, I dunno.
But I laid eyes on her — and her on me — we LOCKED
eyes — and, shit, it was like the fuckin' A-Bomb went off!
I just passed her on the street, understand, just shared a
split-second of eye contact that was the most explosive
thing I ever felt in my LIFE! And you know me, I'm never
impulsive — I just never AM ... but I stopped her and I
said to her, I said, "Do you believe in love at first sight?"
Right there on the street, I stopped her and asked her.
And she laughs, right, she laughs and says, "Yes, I do."
And when she says it, her eyes look into mine, and she
MEANS it, Chas. And I felt, shit, I felt better than that
time I beat Jim Jivinovitch in that State Tournament! A
real high! And we went out that night and the next night
and the night after that — and it was totally MAGIC!
Doing all kindsa stupid, crazy shit like you see in the
movies: dancing to Glenn Miller songs at three in the
morning all alone in the dark, crazy shit! Wonderful
crazy shit! And I kept tellin' myself, "if it all ends
tomorrow, it's been the most magnificent experience in
my life!" But the thing is ... the thing is ... I CAN feel it
ending. That powder-keg that our eyes set-off has already
exploded. It's like a tire losing air real fast and you can't
stop it. And I'm — shit, I guess I'm, like, panicking,
Chas. I don't know how to patch this tire. And I want
more than anything else to patch it. Tell me how, man. I
need somebody to tell me how.

HARVARD BLUES

So the point I'm making here, Russ — can I ... call you
Russ? Just wanted to — all right. Well, my predicament is
such: she's a bit miffed. Mad. Pissed-off? Well, she tells
me I'm too ... intellectual. Yes, Russ. Intellectual. *(beat)*
Exactly what I replied. But not in quite those words.
Which is my point, Russ. Words. It seems to irritate her
that my vocabulary is ... well, more fully developed than
hers is. Now, I can't help Harvard and I can't help the
two years in England, but I think she holds it against me,
Russ, I really do. We get into a discussion about something or other and the usual perfunctory remarks are
bandied about and inevitably it evolves into a debate and
I was always unsurpassed in debate at Harvard, so I
indubitably win every argument by my sheer unavoid-
able ... mastery of the English language. And it's the
English language, Russ, the English LANGUAGE that's
killing my relationship with her. *(beat)* I've tried to tutor
her, or to have her tutored, but she resents it. So that's
why I sought your help, Russ. You ... you really do pump
a *wonderful* tank of gas, but what I'd like you to do is to
teach me to talk like you. A regular guy. Sure, it's a step
down, but ... well, if you knew her, Russ, you'd
understand.

TIT-MAN

I'm a tit-man. Ever since I can remember, I've always BEEN a tit-man. My earliest childhood memories are of having Mom's nipple in my mouth. So I guess you could say that I have a sort of, well, *fascination* with tits. I think about 'em all the time. Well, not ALL the time, but *most* of the time. I'll be doing something — I'll be playing poker or driving my car and they just come flashing into my head. Hundreds of 'em, just popping into my head! It's an uncontrollable thing with me, I can't stop thinking about 'em. I want 'em around me all the time. I drove my last girlfriends away cause I freely admitted I loved 'em for their jugs. This one girl — Carla, I think it was — just about put me in the fuckin' hospital with a baseball bat to my head because I tried to make a plaster of paris imprint of her globes. I dunno exactly WHY I tried to do it now, just that she had the most magnificient tits of any girl I ever dated and I wanted to have a copy of 'em if ever she left me. To, you know, hang over the mantle or something. A memento, to remember her by. Well, she said I was nuts and cracked me across the skull and walked out on me. Can you believe it? Me. Nuts. I compliment her like that, tell her, "I love your breasts, you have the most magnificent breasts of any girl I ever balled," and she walks OUT on me. I dunno, man. I tellya, I can't figure it out sometimes, but I bet if MEN had tits, we'd have a lot more women bangin' OUR doors down. But then again, maybe it's better the way it is. One set of tits in the family is enough. I mean, when you start thinkin' about HIS and HERS bras — it gets pretty ridiculous.

TRAVELS

Don't start name-calling, okay? Just don't start. Let's just remember who hurt who here and keep *that* in perspective, all right? *(beat)* My mind knows it's over. I can stand here and say it's over. For awhile there I couldn't do that. But there's a part inside of me — my heart I guess, whatever you wanna call it — but there's something deep inside of me that still hangs-on to "us." And I know this is not "logical behavior." And I am fully aware that it's been three years now. But you gotta say SOMEthing — DON'T! Do not shut this door in my face. You always said I wasn't ballsy. But I have put a lot on the line coming here like this and I need some kind of response — SOMETHING. Whether it's a "fuck you" or "yes there's room in my life for you now" or — whatever — you can't blow me off this time. You owe me that much. I gotta have some kind of *resolution* here, whether it's good or bad, or else I'm gonna wind up on your doorstep again in a few years or a few months or tomorrow — and I'm gonna be asking the same goddamn thing. I can't ... get *over* this. And I swear to God I've tried. *(beat)* So hit me. Or hug me. Or SOMEthing. I hate to think I blew $200 on plane fare for nothing.

MAN OF ACTION

What it is, George, is an acquired reaction. A basic lesson in learned behavior. Conditioning. Pavlov's dogs. You simply tell someone something over and over again and eventually, they will begin to BELIEVE it. I've been reading all these books, see, and it's TRUE. Incredibly simple but TRUE. No, really. It works. Constant repetition drills it into their thick heads. Elmo, for example. Elmo was the most moronic worker in the whole shop; ran the band saw. Big fat guy? Elmo. Diggs wanted to fire him but I persisted. I said, "let me work with him." So Diggs said okay. And I went to Elmo and I said to him, I said, "Elmo. You can DO this job! You can do it! You can run a BAND SAW!" And little by little, poor old Elmo actually convinced himself he COULD do it! And once he got goin' on that band saw, he was GREAT. *(beat)* Until he cut off his hand. But the point is, he BELIEVED it. That's what you've got to do with Susan. Show her who's boss. Just tell her, "keep cheating on me and you'll be sorry." Tell her. Every time you catch her, tell her again. "You'll be sorry." And eventually, she'll wise-up and stop cheating on you. But you have to ENFORCE your warnings with proof, George. Tell her a half dozen times that she'll be sorry. And if she still persists, hit her in the head with a lug wrench. *(beat)* Times are tough, George. You've got to learn to be a MAN OF ACTION!

IMPULSIVE NATURE

Now I know what you're going to say: that I over-reacted.
I know I might have been wrong but I couldn't help it.
He made me mad. He said something that pissed me off
so I picked him up and threw him out the fucking window. It's only four stories up. No, he didn't die. I looked
out the window and he was kind of crawling away. So I
threw my black and white TV at him. I missed and that
made me madder, so I threw his fucking dog, Charlie,
out the window too. That little rat bastard dog is so light
that he flew all the way across the street and went through
Tommy Petulli's convertible top. Now I gotta deal with
that asshole. I honestly don't think I over-reacted. Once
he ran over me with his brother's Harley when I called
him an asshole. All I did was throw him out the window
when he told me to go fuck myself. I think I was justified.
You know, on his way down I heard him yell, kind of
surprised-like, "you threw me out the fucking window!"
So I said, "Fucking-A right I threw you out the window. I
hope you crack your skull!" It was great.

COLLEGE HILL

You see that porch? It's rotten now ... but my great-grandparents tore those planks up and hid meat under there during the Civil War. Yankee soldiers would come through these little towns and ransack them — steal all the food, burn the houses. But they didn't burn this one. My Grandmother and Grandaddy said fuck you guys and held onto it. Well ... they probably didn't say fuck you, but they DID hold onto it ... It MEANS something. You don't know, you grew-up in a studio apartment, you .... I OWN this! This is mine. And it was my parents' and their parents' and THEIR parents' and before that, it belonged to some Indians I guess. But don't you see? I can't just DROP this place cause a lease is up. I can't do that. If your studio on Central Park South is calling you, then go. But I can't leave this. I ... I *won't* leave this. I know I'm stubborn as hell, I inherited that along with this house. And it IS "all great" here and this house *is* beautiful and this land *is* beautiful ... but what I'm getting at is ... it'd all be even better if you stayed on it.

FOR DAD

I told 'em I wasn't gonna do it. And they just sort of hung their heads and said real soft-like: "Whatever you think is best for you son." It was like something on *Leave it to Beaver,* I felt awful. You can't imagine the guilt, I felt like I had been sunburned all of a sudden, real hot and flushed and nauseous, like that time out at Jones Beach. And I tried to tell 'em what I was feeling. Tried to tell 'em how much I hated it. I told 'em, I said I'd rather die than finish school. But I'm afraid to die, you know, cause I DO believe in reincarnation and if that's the case, I'd grow-up and have to go through school all over again. So I tried to explain how I thought you and me being Roadies and touring all over the country would be good experience. Better experience than this damn military academy that Dad — well, then Dad started crying. I never saw him cry before. I'd seen Mom, sure, but never Dad. And all of a sudden I didn't know WHAT to say so I just said "FUCK!" And I thought he was gonna hit me or something but he just got up and left the room. And I sat there, starin' at Mom, her starin' at me, me feeling like total shit. *(beat)* So I hope you have a good time on the road, Al. I gotta do this one by myself. I gotta do this one ... for Dad.

BOXER'S NIGHTMARE

Look at me! Look at me, all of you! See me for what I am. *(pause)* Please stop lying to me. Please. Every time I've thrown a punch, it was meant to kill. I didn't throw it unless it could do serious damage. I packed a lifetime of hate into every punch. With every punch I hoped to kill, to stop my opponent. To drop him to the canvas. Knock out! It's the only way to survive in my world. I mean, how can you throw a punch just hard enough to knock some-one out but not hard enough to kill him? You can't. You can't. You go in to punch someone's lights out. Whether it's for ten seconds or forever. Now I have. I have punched someone's lights out forever. You know, I felt it. I knew even before I threw the punch. I wound up and reached back into my childhood and let go. I could have stopped it but I didn't want to. I knew it would kill him. Now stop your lying. In my heart I know I murdered a man tonight. Now you can try to call it a lot of other things but I know different. So please, let me live with this.

GOLDFISH

Man, you asked me how we dealt with it, the reality on an everyday basis. We didn't; at least, I didn't — I couldn't. I remember one summer when I was about seven, my parents sent me and my brother to camp through the Fresh Air Fund. You know, one of those programs for city kids. It was wild, all these city kids freaking out on nature and shit. I mean, there were frogs and trees and fucking ponds with tadpoles. Anyway, in the field next to the campsite was this Fireman's Bazaar; they had rides and those booths where you can win prizes — you know, the wheel and the ring toss. Most of the prizes were stuffed animals, but hell, we didn't want no stuffed animals, no teddy fucking bears, we wanted some real nature, a real pet. And in one of the booths you could win a goldfish with its own little bowl. All you had to do was toss a ping-pong ball into the bowl and it was yours. Every night for two weeks we would get three balls for a quarter and toss our asses off for those fish. Never got one. So finally the bazaar packed-up and left and the next day we were in the empty field flinging pieces of carpet around. We walked over to the place where the fish booth was and there lying on the ground was a pile of goldfish. Only they weren't gold anymore. They were all white — with their eyes bugged-out and smelling real bad. We just stared at them for a few minutes and walked away. Never told anyone. So ... that happened. And I had forgotten all about it until one day; I was in-country about a month stationed outside Khe-Sahn. We were out on a sweep where we came across this clearing filled with dead marines. About twelve of them lying across each other.

31

Must have been there five or six days. The heat there can do a number on you. The thing is, I couldn't see their faces. All I could see were those goldfish, all white with their eyes bugging-out and smelling real bad. That's all I could see. In fact, that's *all* I saw during my whole tour. Dead goldfish. So you see, I don't think I ever *really* dealt with it. Not really.

CURE FOR THE CURSE
OF THE LONELY GUY

Don't bury your head in the Froot Loops, Dex! This time it's different! This time — no! — this time, I realized ... Don't tell me you're sick of hearing me talk because I KNOW you're sick of hearing me talk. I'M sick of hearing me talk! Every other day I come home and I'm bursting to tell you about the LATEST WOMAN. "I'm in love, Dex!" "I fell in love on the BUS today, Dex!" or the subway, Dex, or the Flea Market, Dex! Ever since I moved here, I've been torturing myself, allowing myself to FALL IN LOVE with every woman I see! Why? Because I'm a lonely guy, Dex. That's right. And lonely guys make-out well only if they're rich or they look and act like James Dean. And since I'm not or can do neither, I thought, what is the CURE FOR THE CURSE OF THE LONELY GUY? See, Dex, I'm driving down the road and I'm asking myself, "what is the cure for this curse that God or whoever has put upon me?" And that very moment, Dex, as I'm driving DOWN the road, ASKING myself THAT QUESTION — at THAT moment — this MONK crosses the street and I ALMOST ran over him! Missed him by a quarter of an inch, Dex. A quarter of an inch. Do you know just how little a quarter of an inch IS, Dex? Here. That much. And I realized ... yes. I looked at that Monk, lying in the road, and I realized that the Cure for the curse of the Lonely Guy is not to try to be an UNlonely guy, cause he CAN'T be, cause he's already LONELY! The cure, Dex — the cure is to immerse yourself with OTHER lonely guys. *(beat)* So shake my hand, Dex. I joined the monastery.

THE SUGGS SAGA

So. I had a date with this GIRL. Well, I'll get to that in a minute. You know me, I never have a lotta luck with women. But this chick calls me up HERSELF — saw me at the Expo, wants to go out with me. So I figure, sure, okay. So I ask her, what's her name. And she says, Martha Suggs. And I said, "You got a brother?" And she says "No." And I say to her, "this must be fate, see, us gettin' together, cause I went to high school with this guy, good friend of mine, guy named MARK Suggs." I haven't seen him in — what, ten years, but I always liked him. So I told her I'd probably like her. She laughed. Said I was silly. So anyway, I met her at this bar — McHales, you know. And it's a blind date. Sort of. But I KNEW who she was because she LOOKS even like Mark. A little. And I say to her, "so you're not his sister. You're his cousin. You shoulda been straight with me. Told me Mark wanted to fix us up." And I ask her how Mark is these days, and she says, "fine." And I tell her, you know, what great buddies him and me were, and how I'd really like to see him sometime. But she was real ... y'know, *evasive* about him. I thought, maybe he's in some sort of trouble or somethin. But she busted my train of thought by sayin, "would you sleep with me tonight?" And I just about shit in my soup! I mean, I'm no dog, but girls never come up to me on the street and ask me to poke 'em. But I said, "Sure, okay." And I went home with her. And the thing is, I mean, she was GREAT, man, I mean — GREAT. But see, the thing *is* ... she — well, you know, she — she WAS Mark. I didn't find-out 'till the next morning, you know, cause I was really drunk but I went home with her — him — *her*. And we ... DID it. And it wasn't like I did it to a *guy*, you know, he had had an operation, they had changed all the, you know ... PARTS. I mean, he's a WOMAN now. And I started freaking when she told me, but she said, she told me it's really best this way because we were already great friends before we became lovers so it's bound to work-out. *(pause)* I just have no IDEA what to tell everybody when we go back home for our HIGH SCHOOL REUNION.

WOMEN

PRECARIOUS POSITION

Stop right there! Give me back my birth control pills. Ernie, give them back! ERNIE, look at me and read my lips: if you flush those down the toilet, our sex life as you know it will cease to exist. Just slowly hand them over. Ernie, calm down, you're hysterical. I'll tell you what, you give me one pill and you can flush the rest, okay? Just one tiny pill. The one with Tuesday written above it and you can have the rest, okay? Ernie, you're not listening. Ernie! NO! Are you happy? You've had your fun, now give me the rest of those goddamn pills! AAAAAA! Sweatheart, listen, I understand you're hurt. Just give me Tuesday's pill and we'll have a nice, long dinner to disc... ERNIE STOP DOING THAT! Don't you talk to me about trust. You had no business snooping around in my panty drawer. I had those hidden under my garter belt. Ernie, what were you doing with my garter belt? I am not changing the subject. Look honey, I'm just not ready to have a baby. I figured I'd stay on the pill this one last month and then I could get pregnant ... eventually. NO! NOT THAT ONE! NOT TUESDAY! YOU SHIT! THAT WAS THE LAST PACKAGE I HAD! YOU'VE SCREW-ED-UP MY ENTIRE MONTHLY CYCLE. DON'T YOU KNOW THAT SPERM LIVE FOR UP TO 72 HOURS? YOU ASS! If I get pregnant, so help me I'll flush you down the toilet, Ernie. Penis first. And don't you think I won't.

THE SEA OF LIFE

My boss gave me a ticket to the Opera. He buys a season ticket every year and most of the time, he never GOES — he just gives the ticket to somebody in the office, and yesterday, he gave it to me. He's a real lonely person and I think it's sort of sad that he only ever buys ONE seat when he buys season tickets, but I guess maybe he's hoping to meet some EXCITING PERSON sitting next to him — I don't know, but anyway, I took this ticket and went to the Opera. And suddenly ... I found myself in, you know, like, another WORLD. I was sitting on row "B" — that's the second row, Tony — with all the RICH people. And I was looking up at the ceiling, a million miles away and the five balconies towering over my head and the gigantic crystal chandelier as big as your car — it was all so vast and big and beautiful — I felt like a fish in a huge shiny fishbowl. And then the curtain went up into the roof and there was all this glitter and color and SOUND! And I thought about how there's so much more to life than a steady job and a TV set and the JC Penny and the SafeWay. SO MUCH MORE! And that a lot of these rich people sitting around me were probably at one time or another just as poor as me — well, maybe not, but still, what I realized was — WE don't HAVE to stay where we are just cause we're *there!* Like buying a ticket to the Opera, we can jump into new things — DIVE into whole new worlds! It's all out there, Tony. All we gotta do is DIVE IN. I make it sound so easy, but it's scary. Cause as bad as I wanna dive in, I don't want to end-up like my boss and dive-in all alone. *(beat)* So what do you say? You want to go diving? Swimming? In the sea of life?

PICTURE POST CARDS

I didn't never tell nobody this. Maybe cause I never needed to till now. I don't know. This might sound kinda stupid so I'd appreciate it if you didn't laugh. Okay. I came here cause I was lookin' for beauty. My mama used to say Beauty was a horse. See, I seen picture postcards and posters of what folks call beautiful places and I wondered, I always wondered, if maybe they was seein' somethin' I wasn't. You know? Maybe I was missin' somethin'. I only seen one beautiful place in my life. Where I grew up. That little Cracker Box House. Course not to nobody else but me. Silly. Anyway, I figured I'd find one or two more places, beautiful, y'know? It's like I needed to see for myself. So I came lookin'. I think That's a real personal thing, beauty. I really didn't expect to run across a whole new ... idea of what it meant. Or maybe I knew all the time but was runnin' cause I was afraid. Oh gosh, I'm not makin' any sense. Hell, I don't know what I'm tryin' to say except while I was searchin' for beautiful places, I kinda stumbled onto you. You ain't at all what I intended to ... I thought I was lookin' for somethin' to put my finger on. I never felt or touched or spoke to any livin' thing I thought was truly beautiful, what I mean by that word, until I met you. There.

A TRIBUTE TO REAL MEN

Check it out. The guy in the blue. Hairy Chest, cross with Jesus around his neck. See him? Yeah, that's him. He's got a mongo. MONGO, Mongo. This is a nympho dream. Wup — here's another one. Right here on my left. Glasses, Izod shirt? Bananna City. We are in Paradise, Leslie. What are you looking at? Nah, he's a loser. *I know.* You obviously don't know how to pick them. You don't look for pretty little Adonis faces. If you want to know if a man's got the equipment you need, you have to look for specific physical characteristics. Quick lesson: take that guy with Jesus around his neck. Not a classic looker, but virile, masculine, and ten-to-one well hung. Look at the size of his nose. That nose is a tell-tale sign of a truly manly man. See that guy, kinda skinny? Now, look at his head. What gives him away? Hairline. It's receding. The more hair he loses, the more *umph!* he gains. You can't tell by their pants, Leslie, so stop trying. Men are experts at tucking, turning, and stashing away. Detect a bulge? One quick touch — it's gone. Screw the model types. Give me a bald skinny man with a big nose and glasses and I'm set for life. Oh Les! The guy with Jesus is coming over! God, what a gorgeous nose.

PLEASE

Wait a minute, what did you say? No, repeat what you just said. I said, *repeat what you just said! (beat)* I thought that's what you said. I — I can't believe you. I just can-NOT believe you. You want ME to say PLEASE? I ask you to do this for me and you want me to say PLEASE? Here — here I am, frying your goddamn BACON and making your goddamn DE-CAFFEINATED coffee — I am doubled-over with the worst cramps I have ever experienced in my ENTIRE LIFE — I ask you to walk down the block to pick-up some aspirin for me and you want me to say PLEASE FIRST? Well, this is it, buster. This is where I draw the line. This is where the self-centeredness and the one-sidedness stops. Right here. I have put-up with your insults and demands LONG ENOUGH. Fran and Bettice tell me I never assert myself; well I'm doin' it now! You get your ass out of that chair and go down to the SHOP N' SAVE and GET ME SOME GODDAMN ASPIRIN before I throw this skillet full of grease in your lazy good-for-nothing FACE! *(pause)* Please!

STRESS

The doctor told me to be gentle with myself. Isn't that funny? He's scared I'll do the same. But I told him, suicide ain't my bag. He then proceeded to ask me what I remembered about her. I couldn't tell him, but I try to remember the way her feet looked, or how it sounded when she said my name. She used to get up in the middle of the night and eat Hostess Twinkies and then complain about getting fat. She'd pretend she didn't know how it was happening. Sometimes I can hear her. The doctor said that sometimes happens when someone you love dies. And I just want to scream, my mother is not a dead person. That sounds so cold .... I'm scared to look at the grave. It's not so much the dying part, it's me. My insides are so still. Remember right before that tornado in '73? Remember the air was thick and orange. It was so thick it seemed like you had to put your head down just to walk through it. And everything was real, real still. And the birds quit singing, and I remember Dodie wouldn't move. She just laid there with her nose under her paws peering up at me. And all we could do was wait. And then, everything broke. It just broke. And the wind and the lightning and the trees and everything just broke. I remember looking at that funnel cloud like a giant spinning top going through the valley hurting, killing, wrecking. And I remember thinking, there wasn't anything anybody could do. Nothing. I'm scared if I look at that grave, I'll break.

THE PROPOSAL

Look, I really don't make a habit of stopping attractive young men on the street like this, and I realize we just met and I don't even know you very well, but I thought I would ask anyway. *(pause)* Will you marry me? I know, I know. I hear what you're saying. I myself know it is a bit premature. But what the hell, two out of three marriages end in divorce anyway. How much worse could we do? Besides, I'm feeling lucky today. I feel lucky. Yes, I think I might be a little desperate. Well, yes, I am desperate. Okay, okay, what I seem to be getting from you is that you don't want to get married yet. No, hey, that's okay. Really. I understand. I mean, we just met and all that. It's okay, really. How about dinner? Hey, that's okay too, I understand. You don't want to be tied-down. Would you consider lunch? No, you don't want to have lunch, I can tell. Look, I'm sorry. Let's just forget it. Forget I ever brought it up. Let's just forget everything. I'm sorry I put a burden on you. You know, you men never change. You really piss me off. You are so afraid of commitment. Any commitment. I am so tired of this. Are there no real men left?

30 YEARS TOO LATE

Things are so screwed-up in the 80's. Unless you're an in-depth expert in psychology, you can't even go on a DATE anymore. Why? Because you spend the whole time analyzing and evaluating every little nuance — every little *sign* that goes-on. It didn't used to be like that. Men went-out with women and there were understandings and boys liked girls and everybody knew where they stood. But now — this new breed of SENSITIVE MEN! My God, half the time they're either gay or too afraid to initiate anything so you have to spend the whole time DECIDING if you should take the initiative towards any sort of romantic encounter. I mean, whatever happened to romance? And REAL MEN? And Drive-In Movies? And dressing-up for your prom and kissing goodbye on the front steps — in the rain — and dreams and plans for the future? That's what Mom says it was like. Now all there is is fast food and video rentals and gay bars and abortion clinics. *(beat)* I wish I had been a 50's kid. I was just born 30 years too late.

TRUE LOVE

Jake, do you love me? A lot? Do you love me in the animal way? The way animals would kill for their mate? See Jake, I've been doing a lot of thinking as to whether or not I love you and I asked myself, "if anybody ever tried to hurt him, what would I do?" Or how would I feel? And I got this real intense feeling and I realized if anybody ever tried to hurt you, I'd rip their throats out and that's when I knew I must really love you. In the animal sense. Jake, I love you so much; it's just a feeling I get, but remember the other day when that old woman cut in line in front of you and smarted off to you? I almost yanked her teeth right out of her head. I mean, it took everything I had not to pull her cane out of her scrawny little fingers and whack her in the gut. That's how much I love you. When the kids on the corner make fun of your hair — the way it bushes out over your ears — I get so mad. I want to wrap them up in their bicycle spokes. The other day I walked past those little bastards and real calm-like, I bent down to tie my shoe and I took out a razor blade and slashed two of those little shits' tires. They never knew what hit 'em. I love you, Jakey. I knew it when I asked. I said to myself, I said: "Do you really love him?" And when I knew I'd kill for you, I knew I loved you. That's true love, Jake: Love is wanting to kill.

HOT DOG

What the fuck, Simon. It's a HOT DOG. *(pause)* You don't STARE at it, you EAT it. People eat 'em every day, *millions* of people, nobody fuckin' *dies* from it. It's a HOT DOG for chrissakes. Oh, don't give me this shit about "fabricated beef cuts," it's a goddamn HOT DOG for cryin' out loud! Will you just eat it and shut UP about it? *(beat)* Then close your EYES and eat it and shut up about it, okay? Jeez. Okay. Now listen to me: you ever eat pork and beans before? Like when you was in grade school, you had your little plastic tray fulla food and in the little round part you had your pork and beans and in the pork and beans there's these little chunks of somethin' in there? RED chunks? THOSE are hot dogs! Whoever heard of somebody not eatin' a HOT DOG Before? Look, Simon. I know Newlywed life is putting the strain on both of us. You're findin' out things about me you didn't know before and I'm sure as HELL findin' out things I didn't know about YOU before, but we fuckin' learn to COMPROMISE, okay? We try new things and we move the fuck ON! *(beat)* Jesus Christ, I tried SEVEN-TEEN NEW POSITIONS for you last night, will you please just eat the fuckin' son of a bitchin' hot dog for ME? *(pause)* There. Now that's not so bad, is it?

UNEXPECTED

AAAAAAAA! My God! Oh my God! You scared me! Holy shit! Jeez! Oh, I'm sorry. Don't cry. Oh shit, I'm sorry. Please don't cry. It was just — the bandages. I just finished seeing that movie, *Halloween,* and it's late, and I figured you'd be in bed by now. You startled me. With those bandages on your face you look just like the psycho in the movie who kills everybody with a butcher knife. Hey, I'm sorry. You're not ugly. Honest. You're a truly beautiful person inside and as soon as you get those bandages off, you can walk the streets like a normal person. Okay? I mean that. You don't have anything to worry about. You had the best surgeon in town. He does everybody's noses. Okay? Feel better? Good. Now go on back to bed and get some sleep. Oh, and Karen, if you want to wait up for me again? Leave the lights on.

DATING

I am a wonderful person; I know that sounds vain, but I am. I really and truly am. I'm very likable. I hardly ever pitch a fit or raise my voice at people, or animals ... I'm neat and clean and I read all the best-selling books and I've seen every one of Jimmy Stewart's movies and I can recite just about all of Shakespeare's sonnets. I know. I know, I'm coming on too strong here. It's our third date and I'm — I'm scaring you, I can see that. I'm sorry. I just ... we all have FAULTS, right? We all do. Maybe you beat your cat or run-over turtles on the highway or maybe it's not even a spiteful thing — maybe you buy the wrong kind of laundry detergent everytime you go to the grocery store and you kick yourself for not being able to remember. And it's not your fault, you can't remember, you know, and people, you know, come DOWN on you for that. And, well, so I have trouble remembering people's NAMES, okay, it's not like I do it on purpose, it's just my THING ... my one great flaw. And I think you're a really terrific person and I like you a whole lot and who knows, maybe we'll spend the rest of our LIVES together ... for all we know. And I know we've been out three times now and I know you call me every night but — before we go any further ... I have to confess — and don't, like, hate me for this — I CAN'T REMEMBER YOUR NAME!

51

UNEMPLOYMENT

Molly Smith. Smith? Come on, Smith? S-M-I-T-H. Smith. A very American name. Do you speak American? English? Comprehende? Smith is the most American name you can get. Easy to spell too. I apologize, I'm edgy. I'm looking for a temp job, a *temp* job, and I'm a little frustrated with the job market here. I went into the Cafe Tropicana right here in Queens to apply for a job, right? And what's the first question they ask me? "Do you speak Greek?" So naturally, I say, "no, I don't speak Greek, I'm from Kentucky." "Sorry. No Greek, no job." I'm like, what the fuck? I go to a Burger King. This is how desperate I'm getting — a fucking Burger King right here in Queens USA America. "Do you speak Greek?" "No." "Sorry, no Greek, no job." What, do I look Greek with my blonde hair and green eyes? Come on. It was like this every day, every job for a week: retail, diners, receptionists, PET STORES. I mean Christ, I've lived in America every day of my life and I've never had trouble getting a job. EVER! I move here, New York City, Opportunity Capital of the World and I can't get a job because I don't speak Greek or Spanish. All of a sudden I'm the minority. Hell, where I come from if "grits" and "y'all" ain't in your vocabulary you're rode outta town on a rail. You know? I'm not kidding. I ... what? Excuse me? What's my nationality? I have just been telling you for the past half—. American. Americanos? A-M-E-R-I-C-A-N-O-S. I just want my Mom.

SPECIAL

My Mom and Dad used to have these big dinner parties when I was little. And they'd invite all their friends from college to come over. And after dinner, they'd all sit out on the patio and drink red wine and tell all these old stories. And they had this big inside joke, I remember, where one of them would ask Mom what did she do during the "Summer of Love?" And she'd say, "I slept late and *missed* it." And they'd laugh and laugh. I'd laugh too, but I never really knew why. I didn't know what she meant by that. But as I grew older, I came to realize ... I'm a lot like her. Old fashioned. *(beat)* I hope I'm not scaring you, you're giving me the "bank robbery" face again. I'm not trying to wierd you out here, I'm trying to say ... what we're about to do here — or, what I *think* we're about to do here ... it's not just some casual thing that I do all the time like making coffee, y'know? I'm not trying to lay any big philosophies on you, either. I just want you to know that you're very special to me and this ... is a very special thing and I just want you to know ... well, it's sort of been reserved for you. *(beat)* You can stop making a face and kiss me now.

DATE BOOK

I can't believe you did this. I can't beLIEVE it. I — I ought to take this goddamn executive appointment book and cram it down your THROAT! God, Mark. I can't believe you did this. June 6 ... June 15 ... June 29 ... so what am I supposed to do now, huh? Pattern my whole damn LIFE around you? Sit around and wait for these days on your stupid calender to roll around? You can't treat a relationship like a ... Whitman's SAMPLER! Yes you do. You do, that's EXACTLY what you do! Okay, I'll give you a "for instance." I can give you a thousand "for instances!" That time you decided you wanted to "collect" Classical Music? So you ordered Bach's Greatest Hits off that TV ad. and called that your "extensive collection." It's a JOKE is what it is, Mark. I ask you to take me out to dinner. I ask and ask and ask and finally when you DO — we go to the FUCKING WHITE CASTLE! It's HALF-ASSED, Mark! Everything you DO is half-assed! Well not with me, Buster. You are gonna COMMIT to this relationship ... or else ... OR ELSE YOU'RE GONNA BE SITTIN' AT HOME *ALONE* ON JUNE 6, JUNE 15, AND JUNE 29!! *(beat)* And all the REST of these nights too!

FROM THE HEART

I KNOW you want to. And I appreciate it, believe me, I do sincerely appreciate it. But you don't HAVE to. I know it's customary and I know you feel you should, but you really, honest-to-god don't HAVE to! Really! Mom has SO many friends ... they ALL ran-out and did SOMETHING extravagant .... Punch bowls — do you know how many crystal punch bowls I have now? Seventeen. No glasses or ladles to go with them; just the bowls. I have one hundred and nineteen dishes — that's 3½ sets ... 71 forks, 42 spoons, and 9 knives .... eight toaster ovens and three microwaves. I should be opening a restaurant, not getting MARRIED. *(beat)* I've known you since — when? First grade, Peggy? Listen — and I mean it — don't go wasting your money on me. Your blessing is worth more to me than all the Tupperware on the East Coast. And that's from the heart.

MOTHER BY NAME

He's not leaving this house. I don't care what the law says. He's not going back to that woman. I am his mother now. He's growing, he's gained five pounds, he's starting to learn. You should see him. He's allowing his curiosity to ... happen. Everything is starting to interest him. For God's sake, don't take him away now. No! No, you listen to me. When you first brought him to me, he had a bruise covering the entire right side of his face. He was undernourished and he was scared. Every time I walked into a room, he jumped. I'd reach across him at the dinner table for the salt shaker and he'd break into hysterics. He's three years old and every move I make he fears for his life. He's scrapping at three. Every night I sit up with him, holding him, rocking him through his nightmares until he finally sleeps. He never slept when he came here. He sleeps almost all night now. You've got to help me keep this child. He touched my face just this morning — just once, very quickly. One touch. His first touch. I was very still and then I reached out and I touched him. Don't you see how he's mine now? I've nursed that child like a newborn baby, and now you're telling me he goes back? No, I won't let you take him. You'll have to get the National Guard here, honey. I won't let you kill that little boy. And that's what you'll be doing if you send him back there. You'll kill that child. So turn around, go back out the way you came in. And tell your judge, your courts, and that woman — he stays!

PLACE

Ever heard that expression, "caught between a rock and a hard place?" Well, maybe not. It's a ... country expression. I have a lot of phrases like that, phrases you wouldn't understand. And now that I've been *here* all these years, every time I go back home, THEY don't understand half of what I'm saying. It's like ... if you were to take two books ... paperbacks ... let's say, a "how-to" book and a science-fiction book ... and if you were to rip 'em apart — right in half and then glue them back together with each other; the first half of the sci-fi book with the second half of the how-to, and vice-versa; well, then you've got me. You read the whole thing and it doesn't merge together. Hell, I went back there and it broke my heart because I didn't FIT there anymore. And I come back here to you and your coke-spoon-crowd and I sure as hell don't fit in there. So where in the hell do I fit-in, huh? God, this is coming out all wrong. Sounds like some kinda accusation. I'm not accusing anybody. I just wish to hell I had a PLACE that I could call *mine*.

LIBERATED 80'S

WOW! I have never seen so many guys in one place before. Wow! Where are the girls? I mean the ratio here is unreal. I — I'm speechless. I don't know where to begin. There are so many. Cindy, you really know how to pick the hot spots. Not a bit bashful, are they? I mean, look at them, all dancing together. Everybody here seems to know each other. What a great atmosphere. It's so brotherly, huh? God, Cindy, who do I talk to first? Look, look at that, they're all hugging each other. I have found my hangout! My place. Oh, isn't it heavenly to be among men who are so sure of their masculinity they are un-afraid of physical contact with other men? Are you sure this is not a dream? Pinch me. I tell you Cindy, let me write this place down. So I can bring Paula. She will just DIE! The Pink Flamingo? Great! Shit, Cindy. If I don't get picked-up here, I'll sleep with my dog!

PROBLEMS

This is *practically* the same thing. It IS. It is almost practically the EXACT same thing. *(beat)* It's just a step further. A SMALL step further. Look, don't ANALYZE it too much. That's your problem, you know. You over-analyze everything to death. We're not talking about MY problem here. I don't have a problem. We're talking about your problem. Just — listen — just — okay. How long have we known each other? How many intimate serets have we shared? You're closer to me than my own SISTER, Carla. If I could ask my own sister to do this, surely I can ask YOU. It's not my problem, Carla, will you please quit saying that? I don't have a problem. It's you who has a problem. You're blowing this whole thing out of proportion and acting like a martyr, YOU are the one with a problem. I ask you a small favor, what's the big deal, you've done it before, you've done it for me a million times, but no, now it's a big HASSLE! You got a BIG PROBLEM here, Carla. A hundred times you've called-in and told them I was sick, right? So now all of a sudden it's a big deal ... all I want you to do is call in and tell them I QUIT, okay? Why can't YOU handle it? *(beat)* I worry about you, Carla. I worry a lot. Cause if you don't learn to deal with people in a reasonable, direct way, you'll never make it out there.

AND JUSTICE FOR ALL

That's enough! Excuse me, is this or is this not a classroom and isn't making a mistake part of the process called learning? Godammit, I'm talking to you. I don't care what you are, you can't treat your students that way. I won't sit here and listen to your abuse. Just who do you think you are, going off like that? No! I want to know who you think you are! I can't show you respect, sir! I have dug down to the very essence of my being and have yet to discover an ounce, a mere spark of respect. You teach the law of the land. Our justice system. Justice. Fairness. All recitations. Right? RIGHT? No, I won't leave this classroom until I have given my final argument. And I do mean final. I believe in passions and opinions — strong opinions — but I won't listen to your tirades, your verbal abuse of a 21-year-old who happened accidentally to become human in front of a man she very much respected. She made a mistake. You assume the title of teacher, mentor. Assume. You speak of truths, of equality, of fairness. You're the master. No sir. You haven't begun to learn. The word humanity seems to have been omitted from your education, sir. And without that, you're a fraud.

TOO HONEST

Y'know what my problem is? Besides that. I'm too honest. I am, really. You know me well enough by now to know how I always spit-out my deepest, truest, sincerest feelings, whether they're warranted or not. I don't know where I got this from. I sure as hell didn't inherit it — you know Mom and Dad, they're both chronic liars — and incidentally, they *love* you. *I* love you. And I know it's not considered, well, *proper* for us to be seeing each other face to face right before this whole thing, but I feel like, in this particular instance, it's necessary. Because, well ... like I said, I love you and I consider meeting you a regular *miracle* from heaven ... but, I can't marry you. I can't walk down that aisle and say I do because I don't — I CAN'T. I — I'm not ready. And I know this whole thing is supposed to happen in ... 3½ minutes, but in my heart of hearts I have to tell you —I'm not ready for marriage after all. I hope you're not mad at me for telling you this, I'm just being honest. *(beat)* I bet at times like this, you wish I WERE a chronic liar, huh?

PEOPLE

People bug me. I'm not talking about FRIENDS and people that I'm close to. I'm talking about AVERAGE people. You know — the people you see on the BUS; at Penn Station; at the HALF-PRICE TICKET LINE. THOSE kinds of people. Like, the people that read over your shoulder when you're writing a letter on the subway? This morning, I'm riding into the city and I'm sitting there writing a letter to David. And there's this MAN standing over me, holding onto the strap handle, and he keeps READING over my shoulder. Every line I write, he leans over and READS it. And this is a — you know, a very *personal* letter. I can't concentrate on what I'm even writing cause all I can think about is this GUY, standing there, staring at EVERY WORD I set-down on paper! Well, common sense would've told me to just put it away and finish it later. But I must have a revenge streak in me a mile wide; cause I start leading this guy along. I start making the letter real dirty and sexy and I watch him out of the corner of my eye and sure enough, he's following along, reading every single line as I write it and he's getting OFF on it. Damn voyeur. So I keep this up for about 10 lines, getting really, really steamy, telling David about how badly I want him, what I want to DO for him. And this guy is breathing hard now, I can HEAR him. So I take a deep breath and I write — in capital letters — *PRINTED:* I WISH THIS SON OF A BITCH IN THE

POLYESTER SUIT WOULD QUIT READING MY GODDAMN LETTER! He turned SO red ... Got off at the next stop. *(beat)* People are okay, I guess. You just gotta learn how to handle 'em.